Caregiver Reference Guide:
A Handy Place for The Information You Need

Jim Schuster, Certified Elder Law Attorney

Forward

I am often asked by caregivers, elders or their children, "What do I need?" They mean they know they need to get their affairs in order, but don't know what to do. I've put together this handy booklet as a reference guide for anyone to organize and easily find the information they need.

And, we also included some of the "need to know" information for elders, their families and their caregivers. It surprises many people that the caregiving relationship has some many legal implications.

We hope you find this information useful. Let us know if you would want additional information included.

For more copies, just give us a call at (248) 356-3500.

Jim Schuster,
Southfield, MI
2018

AF807903

Table of Contents

Important Numbers

Family

Name________________________________ Phone________________________________

Name________________________________ Phone________________________________

Name________________________________ Phone________________________________

Name________________________________ Phone________________________________

Doctors

Name________________________________ Phone________________________________

Name________________________________ Phone________________________________

Name________________________________ Phone________________________________

Transportation Service

Name________________________________ Phone________________________________

Support Group

Name________________________________ Phone________________________________

Neighbors

Name________________________________ Phone________________________________

Name________________________________ Phone________________________________

Equipment Support

Name________________________________ Phone________________________________

Name________________________________ Phone________________________________

Pharmacy

Name________________________________ Phone________________________________

Veterinarian

Name________________________________ Phone________________________________

Medications

Medication	Strength	How Taken	Taken For

Q & A

Some Quick Questions and Answers

FOR THE CAREGIVER

Does a caregiver need legal advice?

Yes. A caregiver may be making decisions for the care receiver. Those may be medical, financial or others that affect the legal rights of the care recipient. The caregiver needs legal authority to make those decisions.

I am a caregiver for my spouse. Do I still need legal authority?

Yes, each person has his or her own legal rights and interests. For example, you could not substitute for your spouse on his or her job, nor could you call the doctor and make an appointment for your spouse to have surgery because you decided it would be a good idea. If a legal, medical or financial decision must be made and the spouse cannot make it, the caregiver spouse will need to have authority to make the decision.

Isn't it enough to be joint on a bank account?

No. Being a joint owner of a bank account does not give authority to sign a legal document or make a medical decision. For example there could be a dispute over insurance coverage or questions over a recommended course of medical treatment. A joint tenant has no authority to act in these situations.

How does one get legal authority to act?

The caregiver may receive authority from the recipient through powers of attorney for general business and healthcare matters. The alternative is the probate court guardian or conservator. That requires a public hearing after which court may appoint a guardian if it finds the care recipient to be legally incapacitated, or a conservator if it finds the person is under a disability and unable to manage property effectively.

When is a power of attorney the best option?

A power of attorney requires the grantor to have "sound mind." That means that the person has the mental capacity to know what they are doing. If the person is not of sound mind then appointment as the guardian or conservator must be sought from the probate court. The powers of attorney only work where there is trust and confidence in the agent. We would not entrust our life-savings with a person who has an addiction to drugs or gambling. If there is no trustworthy person then appointment of a guardian or conservator would be the best option. That way there is ongoing supervision by the probate court. Between the two methods the powers of attorney cost less, unless the person is indigent in which case the cost of probate court proceedings will be paid by the county.

How may I be appointed guardian or conservator?

A petition must be presented to the county probate court. The filing fee must be paid. The court will appoint a "guardian ad litem," most often an attorney, who will make an investigation and report to the court. The fee will be paid by the elder. The court will hold a hearing to determine whether the elder is so incapacitated that a guardian or conservator should be appointed. The court may appoint an attorney - public administrator. The elder will pay those fees too. If you are appointed then you will receive "letters of authority" and thereafter will be under the supervision of the probate court and report to the court. You may petition for compensation to the court.

What reports must a guardian or conservator make?

A guardian must file annual reports on the status of the "legally incapacitated person." The conservator must find all the property, put it in a conservator account, file an inventory and thereafter file an annual account. The conservator must be prudent with the handling of the property and protect it for the incapacitated person. If a home is to be sold, the conservator must petition the court for permission to sell. The conservator may file a petition with the court for compensation.

May a family Caregiver be compensated?

That depends. If the caregiver is a family member then the law presumes that services are rendered gratuitously. This presumption may be overcome with proof of an agreement to pay. This agreement would have to be in place at the onset of services that are to be compensated. Note, if a nursing home is a possibility within 5 years then Medicaid requirements must be considered. An elder law attorney should be consulted about a Medicaid qualifying personal service contract. A caregiver who is a guardian or conservator will be compensated for those roles, not for being a caregiver *per se.*

Is the Caregiver compensation subject to income tax?

Yes, the "nanny tax" applies to all caregivers who are paid. They fall in the class of domestic household employees. The care recipient is the employer and the caregiver the employee. The employer must withhold income and social security tax and pay the employer's share of social security tax as well as unemployment taxes. The employer should also have workers' compensation insurance in case the caregiver/employee is injured on the job.

Incapacity - No Preparation
Lifetime Probate

If an elder cannot take care of personal business matters because of a medical condition then they may be considered to be a legally incapacitated individual. The probate court can appoint somebody to take of the elder. The process begins with a "petition" filed in court asking for the appointment of a guardian and/or conservator.

Probate Court proceeding. Requires:

- Petition alleging facts supporting incapacity, which means the person is without the ability to care for himself.
- Guardian Ad Litem. The court will appoint an attorney to make an investigation and report to the court.
- Public hearing, not private, in "open court." The evidence presented must detail and prove incapacity.

Guardian

- Makes personal decisions for the Incapacitated Person, such as where to live, what medical treatment to be had.
- Must file an annual report
- Compensation and Expenses are allowed upon court approval

Conservator

- Manages the money and property of the Incapacitated Person
- Must file an Inventory
- Must file an Annual Account detailing all income and expenditures
- Compensation and Expenses are allowed upon court approval

Probate Pro

- Safe way to provide for persons who cannot help themselves
- The only alternative if no trustworthy person to serve as agent
- Provides oversight of those managing an elder's personal and financial affairs
- Provides a forum for resolving disputes
- Decisions are made in public court after all evidence is provided
- Authority of Guardian/Conservator almost never questioned
- Authority can be enforced by Probate Court

Probate Con

- Expensive - court fees, attorney fees, bond and conservator fees
- Slow, cumbersome process, can take months to get a decision
- Public proceedings expose embarrassing private information.
- May not be changed without court approval, hearing will be required

Lifetime Probate Alternatives

Elder law deals in “Life Care Planning” in addition to “Estate Planning.” What’s the difference? Estate planning concerns “death and taxes.” Life care planning concerns our navigation through the aging journey. The goal is to maintain the elder’s independence and control throughout the aging process so that the probate court need not take over the elder’s life. Lifetime probate is thus avoided.

If the Elder has the mental capacity to authorize a trusted person to make medical, legal and financial decisions then he or she can execute documents that empower an "agent" to handle matters. These may encompass all of daily living from paying bills to arranging and managing medical care. But we can also empower the agent to address matters of a complete change in daily living, such as selling the family home and moving into an assisted living facility. Life Care Planning contemplates the best quality of life with dignity and self direction.

Few would disagree that handling medical matters is the most important job an agent can do. So we start with what may be the most important legal document.

Medical/Healthcare Power of Attorney (MPOA)

If an agent is appointed to handle the entire range of medical matters then a Guardian will not be needed. Agents must have the following authority:

- HIPAA. The agent must be authorized to receive confidential medical information.
- MPOA must be immediately effective so Agent can deal with emergencies and routine medical matters without obtaining a doctor's letter of incapacity.
- Designation of Patient Advocate. Under Michigan law a patient can execute a "Designation of Patient Advocate" who will then be empowered to make End of Life Treatment decisions if the patient is unable to participate in informed medical decision making. Two doctors must make the determination of inability to participate. This document takes place of the 'living will.'
- General Healthcare Agent: This agent can handle daily medical matters e.g. doctors' appointments, insurance questions, prescription questions even though the patient could do it

herself

- Mental Health Code. The agent must be given specific authority to make decisions regarding mental health matters such as treatment for depression, anxiety or "agitation."

Recommendation: Everybody must have a complete healthcare power of attorney. Medical treatment has become corporate-insurance driven and very formal. You cannot fully help a patient unless you have a formal healthcare power of attorney.

General Durable Power of Attorney (DPOA)

A general power of attorney is not limited to specific matters such as medical, finances or real estate. While it is possible to have a durable power of attorney limited to finances, it is better if it is general. For the range of business of an elder it is most efficient, and most economical, to have a "general" power of attorney. The term "durable" means it is still effective even after the "principal" is incapacitated.

Here are points to address when contemplating a durable power of attorney:

- Specific Authority. An agent, sometimes called "attorney in fact" can only handle matters that are expressly authorized, nothing else.
- Requires Trustworthy person
- Extraordinary powers - self dealing, gifting, employing and compensating family members, establishing a trust and so on are needed for Asset Protection and must be expressly given.

To be fully effective the DPOA should grant complete powers concerning all business elder has including:

- Pension Plans, IRAs
- Real Estate, investments, Stocks/Mutual Funds
- Annuities, Insurance
- Government Benefits
- Trusts
- Credit Cards
- Applying for government benefits and the accompanying gifting and asset transferring powers. The agent will also need the power to "self-deal."

Pros & Cons of the DPOA

Pro

- Inexpensive
- Elder remains in control, grants permission to another to act
- May be changed or revoked at a ny time

Con

- Can be tool of elder abuser
- Requires reliable and trustworthy person to serve as Agent
- Service is voluntary, Agent is not required to act
- If elder is incapacitated, is unable to supervise
- Can be rejected by providers, especially "Wall Street" investment companies

Recommendation: Everybody must have a general power of attorney. Without it you cannot take care of all business of another person, even your spouse.

Using the General Durable Power of Attorney

There are many reasons for having a Durable Power of Attorney, and not all of them are related to the possibility of becoming incapacitated. A complete and immediately effective durable power of attorney authorizes the "agent" to take care of all identified business. Not just any document will do. For example it should address: banking both opening and closing accounts; insurance including purchase, claims and redemption; credit including opening and closing accounts; presenting claims for private and government benefits and contesting denials of benefits. This is why it is important to have trusted individuals appointed as Agents and to have the document effective immediately.

Often a family member or other person is added to accounts for convenience purposes, so they can write checks and assist the account owner when they need to transact business. Two of the possible risks in this situations are 1) if the co-owner is in a collections situation. The joint accounts may be found and it may be difficult to protect them.2) any account that a potential Medicaid applicant's name is on is considered their account by the Department of Human Services. In both these situations, having a Durable Power of Attorney in place for the owner of the accounts will avoid the problem.

The second common reason co-owners are added to accounts is to avoid probate. The intent is for the survivor to have the account at the death of the owner. This can be easily accomplished by designating a beneficiary for the account.

The first step once the Durable Power of Attorney has been completed and signed is to present it to all of the financial institutions where the principal holds accounts and have it put on file. If a period of time passes between the execution of the document and presenting it to the institutions, they may question if it is still valid. The Agent's powers do not necessary take immediate effect, but everything is in place if needed.

When acting as Agent, always, always, always, sign as Agent. Any of the following ways are acceptable:

Jane Doe by her Attorney-in-Fact, John Smith

Jane Doe, by John Smith, Agent

Jane Doe, by John Smith, POA

If the signature does not make it clear you are signing under the authority of the Durable Power of Attorney, you are signing as yourself and may become personally responsible for the terms of whatever agreement is involved. When signing as Agent, you are actually signing for the principal of the Durable Power of Attorney.

Keep careful records of all actions taken when acting as Agent, save all documents and receipts, and remember the duty is to act in the best interest of the principal. There is the potential for serious penalties for misusing the authority of the Power of Attorney in a manner that is knowingly harmful to the principal and for the benefit of the Agent.

Using the Healthcare Power of Attorney

The Healthcare Power of Attorney is a multipurpose document. It's first purpose is to appoint Patient Advocates to speak for the patient whenever the patient wishes the advocate to deal with something, including when the patient is unable to speak for her/himself. This includes discussing the patient's case with doctors, nurses, insurance companies, and other care providers. The Patient Advocate may be a family member but does not need to be. The most important points to consider when choosing a Patient Advocate are trust and their understanding of your end of care wishes.

Immediately Effective: The Healthcare Power of Attorney should be effective immediately. A patient advocate needs to be able to act in case of emergency without any prior conditions such as seeking two doctors' letters that the patient is "unable to participate in medical decisions."

HIPAA: The Healthcare Power of Attorney includes a HIPPA release which allows the Patient Advocate access to any medical records necessary as well as gives all health care providers permission to speak to the Patient Advocate regarding the patient's care, medical decisions, billing and insurance issues.

Mental Health Code: A Healthcare Power of Attorney drafted to current State of Michigan guidelines addresses the patient's wishes regarding mental health care. If it does not address mental health, the Patient Advocate has no authority to make decisions regarding mood medications and psychiatric treatment.

Advance Directive: The most sensitive section of the Healthcare Power of Attorney is the Advance Directive, or Living Will. Nothing can replace discussing your feelings about end of life care with your trusted Patient Advocates. Talk about the experiences of family and friends, even stories on television and in movies and think about what your choices would be in various situations. Many people are very firm in their belief that they never want to be on a ventilator and include that in their Advance Directive. They are not aware that a ventilator may be used for a brief period during and after certain procedures and is temporary in those situations.

There are often religious guidelines that you may want to incorporate into your Advance Directive. It is important to appoint Patient Advocates who understand and respect them regardless of their own beliefs. Your document may include a reference to your choice of spiritual advisor for your Patient Advocate to consult should they need more detailed guidance.

The Advance Directive is a very important, very personal document, and may include or exclude anything you wish. It should also be updated as necessary with changes in your choices of Patient Advocate and your decisions regarding your Advance Directive.

Patient Advocacy

The advocate must "manage" the patient's care. That means being fully advised of the current treatment plan and making sure it is fully carried out. It means asking questions. It means being vigilant for problems not being treated such as a developing bedsore or reaction to a new medication. It means talking to staff and the doctor about treatment issues. It means getting your patient to emergency if serious medical problems are not immediately addressed.

Good care requires active management of the delivery of healthcare. Remember: You are the boss. You are employing them to provide care to your patient.

Whether you are acting for the patient in home, in hospital or in a nursing home you need to be informed. In any setting you must know the patient's rights and actively exercise them. In home, hospital or nursing home that means knowing the patient's rights and benefits under Medicare.

The Patient Advocate and the Rights of the Medicare Patient

Even if the resident did not enter a nursing home from the hospital, the patient advocate must be knowledgeable about Medicare processes. A long term nursing home resident may have trips to the hospital. When the resident enters the nursing home on a post-hospital skilled care stay, the quality and completeness of treatment may dictate how well the patient does. Sometimes the patient returns home only through the vigorous advocacy of the patient advocate. The patient advocate is essential to the patient receiving quality care.

If you are helping an elder you must be an informed advocate. Perhaps the most important arena for that advocacy is in the medical field. Elders and a few others remember the days when it was just the patient and the doctor. It used to be you could call and speak with the doctor who might say "take two aspirins and call me in the morning." And, who remembers that you actually could call the doctor the next morning! Those same folks remember when doctors had "admitting privileges" or were "on staff" with a local hospital and the doctor would actually visit you in the hospital. No more, those days are gone!

Medicine has gotten extremely complicated. Your doctor does not do it all anymore. There are prescriptions that only specialists can administer and oversee. When you go to the hospital, you will not see your doctor there. You will have an "attending physician" who will coordinate with the specialists who may be part of the treatment team. Here are some of the issues in advocacy you need to know about.

Medicare

- Premature Termination of Skilled Care. A patient's "skilled care" such as post hospital "rehab" should not be terminated merely because a patient stopped "making progress." It should be continued if merely to maintain function.
- Improper Discharge -

Nursing Home Advocacy

- Learn about dangers of antibiotics with an elderly patient and learn the warning signs.
- Learn about the dangers of mood medications (psychotropic) that are often prescribed with a resident is "agitated."
- Learn about the dangers of changes in electrolyte levels
- Know the warning signs of deadly reaction to medications
- Weight loss is a sign of declining health, find out what is going on.
- Be on the lookout for decubitus ulcers (bedsores) and monitor treatment

Compensating the Caregiver

Of all the problems that arise when an elder needs personal assistance with daily matters, perhaps the least recognized are those that arise when a caregiver is compensated. This includes both private and family caregivers, but not commercial agencies. These issues become more complex when the caregiver handles the elder's finances and compensates herself.

Employer & Employee

Under the laws of most states when a person is paid for caregiver services, an employer employee relationship is created. Being an employer creates a host of legal duties and responsibilities. These are not avoided by claiming the caregiver is an "independent contractor." The employer-employee relationship is defined and controlled by law.

How does the law determine whether the caregiver is an employee or an independent contractor? Perhaps the best guide is found in IRS Publication 15a. It lists some 20 factors to consider. In general in-home personal services are presumed to be supervised. Examples of unsupervised in-home services include the work of tradesmen such as a plumber or electrician.

Is the child the employer if she hires someone to take care of her parent? If a child acts for the parent by oral authority or a power of attorney and directly hires the person, then the elder is the employer. If the child chooses, hires and pays a person to perform caregiving service for a parent, then the child is the employer. If an agency is hired then the agency is the employer.

Duties of the employer

Legal Employee

You must have proof the person you employ is legally able to work. You need to have a completed U.S. Citizenship and Immigration Services (USCIS) Form I-9, Employment Eligibility Verification in your file.

Employment Discrimination laws

Employment Discrimination laws commonly ban discrimination based on race, age, sex and other factors. While the federal law only applies to employers over a minimum number of employees, you may be subject to state or city anti-discrimination laws.

Minimum wage

Check and see what the minimum wage is in your area.

Employment taxes

If you pay any one person more than $2,100 per year, you are responsible for FICA taxes and those are Social Security and Medicare taxes. The employer is also responsible for withholding the employee's share of those taxes. Currently the total tax rate is 15.3%. If the employer does not withhold and pay the tax the IRS will impose penalties, interest and proceed to collect from the employer.

The employer is responsible for withholding income tax from the employee. The employer may be relieved of this duty if the employee fills out a "W9" form indicating the number of dependent deductions results in no tax due. You should check your state income tax requirements.

Federal and State Unemployment Compensation

An employer is also responsible for paying unemployment taxes. A terminated or laid off employee may be able to collect unemployment compensation on the employer's account.

Failure to pay taxes

An employer who fails to pay required taxes may find that the penalties and interest equal the amount of taxes owed.

Workers Compensation

What if the caregiver injures her back or knee helping lift the elder? What if she falls down the stairs and fractures a bone? She can file for workers compensation to cover her medical expense and her wage loss. Your homeowners' insurance will likely not cover employees. You should have workers compensation insurance.

While the list of employer requirements looks formidable it can be easily met if you consult an accountant use a payroll service.

Other issues

Completing the duties of an employer is not the end of considerations when compensating caregivers.

Government Benefits

If the care recipient is a wartime veteran or a surviving spouse of an eligible vet then caregiver payments will be a factor in eligibility for VA "Aid and Attendance" pension benefits. The VA considers such payments to be "unreimbursed medical expense" where the need for services are caused by a medical condition, which must be supported by medical evidence.

Unlike the VA, many state long term care Medicaid programs presume that payments to caregivers were made to qualify for benefits. The Medicaid program only allows an applicant to have $2,000 of cash assets and has a five year "look back" or review of financial transactions made within time period. In many states the payments are deemed "divestment of assets" which means the payments were transfers of assets for less than fair market value, made for the purpose of qualifying for Medicaid benefits. This conclusion can be avoided with advance planning. For example the Michigan Medicaid program requires a certification of need for the services by a doctor and a personal service contract that conforms to the

Medicaid agency's requirements.

Child Caregiver Compensation Issues

Compensating a child brings additional legal issues. This compensation includes not only pay for service, but can include gifts of cash or property to the child.

It helps to understand the issues concerning child caregivers if one keeps foremost in mind the legal presumption that children should not be paid for helping parents. Under the general law children are presumed to provide commercially valuable services for free, for "love and affection." It does not matter how valuable the services are or how much a parent was paying for the same service before the child began to help.

Even if the child is not paid, any unaccounted loss or use of the parent's money may be presumed to have been taken by the child. A parent may have agreed to the child's taking of the money as a gift. However, if the parent suffers from cognitive decline or memory problems she may not remember making the gift and the child will face legal consequences.. There must be evidence that the parent understood what the payment was for and that the parent freely consented to the payment. Oral consent is not enough.

Caregiver Child is a "Fiduciary"

In short a "fiduciary" is a person trusted to handle the affairs of another and in this article we address the caregiver's handling the financial affairs of the elder. An elder may have very haphazard record keeping of finances. But, when a child is trusted to take care of all the parent's business, the child is a "fiduciary." The child is held to a high standard of conduct such that all actions may only benefit the parent. If the caregiver fails to meet the standard he or she will be responsible for any harm or loss the parent suffers. How does a person meet the high standard?

When the child handles the parent's finances, complete and detailed records must be kept. For example many elders still like to have cash in the home to make payments. It saves them trips to the bank. If the caregiver is managing the finances the practice is risky unless the monthly cash withdrawals are modest. Otherwise the caregiver may have no record of where the money went and as a fiduciary be responsible for any loss. It may be presumed that the caregiver took the money.

Mom Leaves the Nursing Home

A hypothetical may provide a useful context to show how problems can develop. Suppose a parent is in a nursing home, is paying $8,000 a month and receives horrible care. Suppose a daughter steps up and provides 24 hour care for her mother in her home and Mom does much better. By any commercial measure the daughter is providing care worth more than $8,000 a month. After six months the daughter is exhausted and her mother, who has memory problems, agrees that daughter should have a nice vacation. Daughter arranges for mom's care in the home and goes on a great Las Vegas vacation at a cost of $10,000 out of mom's bank account. Mom does fine, daughter comes back and brother who never offers to help finds out about the expensive vacation. Mom does not remember agreeing or the payment. What could happen?

Elder Financial Abuse

The brother could file an elder abuse charge. If a child has control of the parent's finances and takes payment out of the account, without proof of informed consent by the elder, then the child may be accused of theft or elder abuse. This can result in criminal charges.

Control of Parent

The brother may hire an attorney and file a guardianship petition for control of the parent and the parent's money. This can be a whole article in itself, but in short it can be very expensive and the elder may end up footing the bill. If the court grants the petition it may not appoint either child as guardian. The court may take the elder under its continuing supervision with an attorney or professional guardian managing the parent's affairs. That guardian may remove Mother from the home, place her in a nursing home and demand a full accounting from the daughter. That can start a series of court expensive actions.

Inheritance

What if the mother makes a Will favoring the daughter for providing care for her? Major court battles can erupt after a parent dies. If a child receives more than the others, through the Will or a joint bank account, expect the "knives to come out." The siblings will hire attorneys and begin court action. Where a child has had significant time alone with the parent and control of the parent's finances, the favored gift may be overturned by the court.

The Will can be contested on grounds of "undue influence" which means the child used his or her position to make the parent decide to give the caregiver a larger share of the estate. The greater the need for a full-time caregiver the easier it is to prove undue influence or elder abuse. If the will contest is successful the caregiver will not get the gift and could end up with an even smaller share of the estate.

Even without charges of undue influence, lifetime payments or gifts may result in a probate court contest. A court may rule that the money is an advance on inheritance leaving the caregiver with a diminished share of the estate and no recognition for the years of service that the child may have rendered.

Recommendation

This article has not exhausted the "What if" scenarios that can occur in the caregiver - elder context.

When the caregiver - elder relationship is begun there must be an agreement on the terms and conditions of the caregiving relationship. What about compensation? Even if government benefits are not contemplated a legal contract is a good idea.

And finally, while the parent's "business" is her own private affair, when a child is a caregiver a family meeting at the outset is simply wise.

Be prudent, be safe. Talk to an elder law attorney and make sure you "do it right."

Caregiver Contract

The caregiver contract is a solution to the problems presented.

- Agreement made at onset. All family involved
- Contract on services, frequency and compensation
- Assessment made of services needed and Fair Market Value of those
- Medical support/proof must be obtained to determine need
- Contract must comply with tax and employment laws
- Terms Must Satisfy VA and Medicaid requirements
- Avoids financial elder abuse allegations

Criminal Punishment for Caregivers Who Abuse Their Power

We all know that a caregiver is in a position of power over an elder who needs the help. Naturally many laws apply to the relationship that help the elder.

A caregiver can intentionally or mistakenly violate the law. It is easy to see how the law can be violated. After a caregiver is hired we start to notice a parent's valuab les are missing. A child moves into the parent's home and lives high on the parent's money while she is left in bed unkempt, filthy, and close to starving.

But there are also borderline cases. A daughter moves in to help a parent who has Alzheimer's disease. After many months of 24 hour care, the daughter finds she needs to get a job to get her car repaired and pay her maxed out credit cards. She waits for a good time when Mom is of clear mind. She tells Mom that she needs to get a job and feels very badly since Mom cannot be home alone may have to move out of her home to an apartment. Mother is shocked and asks is there anything she can do. After much discussion Mom agrees to help her daughter get her car fixed and credit cards paid off. Daughter writes the checks. Early the next month, oldest brother comes over for a visit and checks the bank statements as he always does. He is shocked to find thousands of dollars in checks from Mom's account. He immediately goes to Mom and asks "What's going on here?" Mom doesn't remember a thing. Brother is outraged. "Mom, your daughter is stealing from you!" He hires a lawyer and they file charges against sister.

In this hypothetical, Daughter was incredibly foolish in not talking with other family members. But, did she commit a crime?

Here are various Michigan crimes that apply in the elder/caregiver context. Note, this is not a complete list. MCL refers to Michigan Compiled Laws.

Vulnerable Adult Abuse, MCL 750.145m, n

The statute includes a caregiver who directly cares for or has physical custody of a vulnerable adult. The crime is complete when knowingly commits an act that causes serious mental harm or one that poses an unreasonable risk of harm or injury to a vulnerable adult, regardless of whether physical harm results.

Embezzlement, MCL 750.174

A caregiver who has control of a bank account and takes money for her own use without consent of the elder can be guilty of embezzlement. An elder who has Alzheimer's may lack the capacity to consent to the use of the money.

Extortion, MCL 750.213

While the daughter hypothetical may not support a charge of extortion, caregivers who isolate elders from their family have been known to use threats to get money from the elder.

Forgery MCL 750.249.

If without knowledge of the elder, a caregiver signs the elder's name to a check for her own benefit may be guilty of forgery.

Michigan the Identity Theft Protection Act: MCL 445.61.

A caregiver who uses the elder's personal identifying information to obtain money or credit for the caregiver's personal use violates the law.

Unauthorized credit application, MCL 750.219e.

A caregiver who submits an application for a loan or other extension of credit in the elder's name without authorization from that other person. This can happen when a caregiver executes a plan to get money from the elder by a home equity loan.

Using a computer to commit a crime, MCL 752.796

Using a computer to commit another crime is an additional violation of law. For example commission of unauthorized credit application by computer would be violation of both laws.

Obtaining Money or property by False Pretenses MCL 750.218

A person who uses fraud to obtain money or property. For example misrepresnting what a check is for and then obtaining the elder's signature falls under this crime.

Larceny, MCL 750.357

Simple theft is called larceny.

Assault and Battery MCL 750.81

This is the common crime of physically striking a person.

Government Benefits

The following programs are administered by the VA, "Veterans Administration."

Disability Compensation

VA Compensation benefits are for those veterans injured during service. The amount of the cash benefit is determined by the percentage rating. (see below) This program does not consider the veteran's net worth or financial need.

- Disability must be service connected, can be aggravation of existing condition.
- Vietnam Veterans who served "in country" are presumed eligible if they have prostate or respiratory cancer; ischemic heart disease; Parkinson's disease, and some other conditions. See the VA for more information.
- Veterans Stationed at Camp Lejune 30 days or more during 1950s - 1980s and have a presumed condition such as a cancer are eligible. See VA for more information.
- A Claim can be made years after service, such as hearing loss of WWII Vet.
- Rating may be increased if condition worsens over years.
- May receive additional Special Monthly Compensation if housebound or require the aid and attendance of someone to perform daily living functions.
- Benefits are non-taxable and are not based on income or net worth.

Compensation Rate Table

Rating %	10 %	20 %	30 %	40 %	50 %
Veteran Alone	$136.24	$269.30	$417.15	$600.90	$855.41
Veteran with Spouse	$136.24	$269.30	$466.15	$666.90	$937.41
Rating %	60 %	70 %	80 %	90 %	100 %
Veteran Alone	$1,083.52	$1,365.48	$1,587.25	$1,783.68	$2,973.86
Veteran with Spouse	$1,182.52	$1,481.48	$1,719.25	$1,932.68	$3,139.67

Special Improved Pension

The pension program is a needs based program for aged or disabled veterans. It considers the veteran's income and net worth in the approval, denial and calculation of benefit. In addition the veteran must have served during wartime, though the disability need not be related to service. The qualifying service dates are:

World War II:	12/07/1941 - 12/31/1946
Korea:	06/25/1950 - 01/31/1955
Vietnam in-country:	02/28/1961 - 08/04/1964

Vietnam era: 08/05/1964 - 05/07/1975

- "Disabled." Age 65 and up qualifies as being disabled.
- Provides cash, tax free, support for "Unreimbursed Medical Expense" (UME).
- To be deducted, medical expenses must exceed 5% of Maximum Annual Pension Rate (MAPR).
- UME not only includes uncovered medical or pharmacy bills, but also includes paid help that an aide provides with personal needs such as bathing and other "ADLs" (Activities of Daily Living). Payment to family members for assistance qualifies as UME.
- UME includes the cost of necessary residential care for a Vet with a cognitive conditions such as dementia. If the Vet needs a safe living residence such as a "Memory care unit" in "assisted living" facility, the expense is UME.
- Maximum benefit when UME is equal or greater than monthly income.
- Asset ("net worth") limited program. Net worth may be reduced by transferring assets.
- Three Year "look back" on property or "asset" transfers made to reduce net worth.
- VA benefit planning may conflict with Medicaid, which has a 5 divestment occurs within 5 years of application a "penalty period" will be imposed. During this time Medicaid will not pay nursing home or MiChoice waiver benefits. The period can be avoided if all assets are returned prior to application.
- The VA no longer allows purchase of an annuity within the 3 year look back to reduce net worth.

Maximum Annual Pension Rate (MAPR) (2018)

Veteran Surviving			**Surviving Spouse Pension**		
Status	Annual	Month	Status	Annual	Month
Service Pension - Veteran	$13,166	1097	Basic pension	$8,830	736
Veteran + 1 Dependent	$17,241	1437			
Housebound Veteran	$16,089	1341	Housebound	$10,792	899
" " + 1 Dependent	$20,166	1681			
Aid & Attendance Veteran	$21,962	1830	Aid & Attendance	$14,113	1176
" " + 1 Dependent	$26,036	2170			

Annual Benefit: increase or refund to VA

The Pension benefit is calculated on an annual basis, that is benefits are awarded per benefit year. A veteran whose income is lower or UME is higher may seek an increase in benefits if not at the maximum. At the end of the year, expect the VA to review the recipients received income and UME. The VA will also review the recipient's tax records for the amount of reported income. If income were more or UME less than the amount expected, the VA will seek refund.

VA Health Care Benefits

The Veterans Healthcare Administration (VHA) also offers in-home benefits. The vet must be enrolled in VA Healthcare (VHA) to receive those. These benefits must be the result of an individual treatment plan determined by VHA medical team. Contact your VA hospital/facility to learn about program availability. These are some of benefits:

Community Adult Day Care

Benefit provides social interaction for vets who need assistance with activities of daily living.

Home Health Aide

Provides medically necessary services including assistance with ADLs and household tasks to maintain safe living for veteran. Program may be used for respite for vet's caregiver. VA uses private contractors to provide from 2 to 42 hours per week.

Veteran Directed Care

This benefit provides cash payment for non-agency aides to Veterans at risk of nursing home placement. Vet hires aides, may be friends or family, to provide home care services so the vet can live independently in-home.

Veterans Information

Here is where you can get more information on VA programs and assistance in getting documentation needed for program benefits.

Veterans' Services Oakland County	248-858-0785
Veterans' Services Wayne County	313-224-5045
Veterans' Services Macomb County	586-469-5315
Veteran Service Organizations - Detroit list (includes VFW, Amercan Legion etc)	https://levin.house.gov/resources/veterans
To Request Military Records Contact Your	Local Veterans' Services Office or

http://www.archives.gov/veterans/military-service-records/get-service-records.html

Long Term Care - Medicaid

Medicaid is a federal program administered by the State of Michigan. It is "means tested." That means an applicant must meet asset and income limits. Michigan has two long term care programs. The MiChoice Waiver provides part-time, long term care services in the person's residence. It has asset and income caps. The nursing home program pays for full-time care and has the same asset limits but no income limit.

Medicaid In-Home -- "MiChoice" Medicaid Waiver

This program is administered by the Area Agencies on Aging and a few other agencies. The goal of the Medicaid Waiver program is to enable recipients to live in their own residence and minimize institutional care. However the program has limited openings, "slots", and these are allocated according to service priority. The two highest are those who are in a nursing home, the nursing facility transition initiative (NFTI) and those whose medical condition puts them at "imminent risk" for nursing home placement. Applicants with lesser needs may have significant waiting periods.

- "Medicaid Waiver" has all asset rules of Nursing Home Medicaid
- Is income capped. If income is more than $2,199 may not receive benefit
- Program provides services such as personal care, home delivered meals, private duty nursing, housekeeping and transportation.
- Program will not provide total support or 24 hour care
- May be coordinated with and supplement VA benefits
- It is subject to after death "Medicaid Estate Recovery" (can be avoided)

Medicaid - Nursing Home

- Must need nursing home level of care
- "Spend Down" to $2,000 of "countable assets"
- Applicant must be in a nursing home "Medicaid Bed"
- Applicant and spouse allowed "exempt assets" e.g. home, car, funeral plan
- At home spouse is allowed to keep half of "countable assets" to a maximum of $123,600. Any more than that must be either be spent down or "sheltered."
- Assets of married and single applicants can be "sheltered" ("asset protection")
- 5 year "look back" on "divestment" (gifts)
- It is subject to after death "Medicaid Estate Recovery" (can be avoided)

Excluded Assets and Countable Assets

Assets of applicants are sorted into two categories. Excluded assets include a home, personal possessions, vehicle and funeral plan. Countable assets include everything else that could be reduced to cash. Countable assets must be spent down.

Medicaid "Spend Down"

In 2018 single Medicaid applicants must "spend down" their "countable assets" to $2,000. Married couples may save up to $123,600 more of countable assets for the "Community Spouse Resource Allowance. Countable assets are those that can be reduced to cash. Applicants may spend on anything for themselves, their spouse or their property. They may purchase new items, fix or repair current property.

Medicaid Estate Recovery

Long term care Medicaid comes with "estate recovery" which means the recipient must pay back the government the amount of benefits paid out. It does not matter whether the recipient paid a lifetime of social security and income taxes. The pay back is collected out of the deceased recipient's probate estate. If probate is avoided the government recovers nothing. A "Lady Bird" deed avoids probate and Medicaid Estate Recovery, under the current Michigan program.

Useful Terms

ADLs	Activities of Daily Living-eating, bathing, dressing, toileting, mobility
Adult Protective Services	Division of the Department of Human Services that investigates possible financial, mental, or physical abuse of adults.
Advanced Directive/ Living Will	Document detailing an individual's wishes for end of life medical care.
Agent/Attorney in Fact	Person named in Durable Power of Attorney to manage the Principal's financial affairs as necessary
Alzheimer's Disease	Progressive brain disorder that gradually causes loss of memory and ability to learn, communicate, and carry out daily activities. It may also cause personality and behavior changes.
Assisted Living	Residential facility for individuals who need assistance with the activities of daily living, but do not require 24 hour care. These facilities are not licensed for Medicare or Medicaid.
CMS	Centers for Medicare and Medicaid Services
Care Plan/ Treatment Plan	A written plan outlining treatment goals and services to be provided by the professional caregiving team.
Conservator	Person appointed by the court to manage and protect an incapacitated individual's finances.
Dementia	A loss of memory and other mental abilities severe enough to interfere with daily life. Can be caused by a number of conditions, including Alzheimer's, Huntington's, Parkinson's, and vascular diseases as well as strokes, and other disorders.
DHHS	Michigan Department of Health and Human Services-administers Medicaid Programs among many others.
DNR	Do Not Resuscitate Order signed by the doctor and the patient
DPOA (Durable Power of Attorney)	A legal document appointing persons to sign documents and perform identified transactions on one's behalf
Elder Law	Legal field concerning issues of aging, such as estate planning, powers of attorney, wills, and government benefits.
Fiduciary	Anyone who holds the assets of another and has the duty to make financial decisions on behalf of another person

Grantor/Settlor	Person who establishes a Trust
Guardian	Person appointed by the probate court to manage an incapacitated individual's personal affairs, such as medical care and living arrangements.
HIPPA	Health Insurance Portability and Accountability act of 1996; among other things protects the patient's right to privacy
Hospice	Services that provide comprehensive care for terminally ill patients and their families, focusing on comfort.
Level of Care	Amount of assistance required by an individual; used by Medicaid to determine need for nursing home care.
Living Trust	This trust is created during a person's lifetime, avoiding probate for all assets that are owned by the trust.
MPOA	Medical Power of Attorney-legal document appointing Patient Advocate
Nursing Home	State licensed facility that provides 24 hour skilled nursing care.
Patient Advocate	Person named in Healthcare Power of Attorney to make medical decisions when the Principal is incapacitated
Personal Representative	Individual named to execute a will; formerly called the executor
Representative Payee	Person chosen by the Social Security Administration to manage an incapacitated individual's Social Security benefits
Skilled Care	Higher level of care that may only be performed by skilled medical personnel such as rehabilitation, injections, dressings, etc.
Snapshot Date	Date of first admission to hospital and/or nursing home for at least thirty continuous days
Spend-down	Term used by the Department of Human Services referring to the process of reducing a Medicaid applicant's assets to an eligible level. It does not necessarily mean actually spending the applicant's funds, assets can be sheltered.
Trustee	Person or institution appointed by the Grantor to be the manager, following the directions contained in the document.
MiChoice Waiver Program	One of many terms for a Medicaid program that may provide home-based assistance.

Important Documents

☐ Driver's License/Health Insurance/Social Security/Medicare Cards	Location
☐ Durable Power of Attorney	Location
Agent_	Successor Agent
Phone_	Phone
☐ Health Care Power of Attorney	Location
Patient Advocate_	Successor Patient Advocate_
Phone	Phone
☐ Living Trust	Location
Trustee	Successor Trustee_
Phone	Phone
☐ Will	Location
Personal Representative	Successor Personal Representative
Phone	Phone
☐ Guardianship Paperwork	☐ Conservatorship Paperwork
☐ Long Term Care Policy	Location
☐ Deed(s)	Location
☐ Life Insurance Policies	Location
☐ Homeowner's Insurance Policy	Location
☐ Car Insurance Policy	Location
☐ Stock Certificates	Location
☐ Savings Bonds	Location
☐ Burial Plot Paperwork	Location
☐ Prepaid Funeral Paperwork	Location
☐ Veterinarian Records for Pets	Location
☐ Duplicate Keys	Location

□ Vehicle Titles	Location
□ Safety Deposit Box	Location

Checklist: Is it Time for a Nursing Home?

A simple review of the Activities of Daily Living for persons in the home

	From Independent – to –		Totally Dependent	
Housekeeping	0	1	2	3
Recognizes Strangers	0	1	2	3
Driving	0	1	2	3
Social Interactions	0	1	2	3
Getting Groceries	0	1	2	3
Eating	0	1	2	3
Recognizes Surroundings	0	1	2	3
Following Instructions	0	1	2	3
Wandering	0	1	2	3
Personal Hygiene	0	1	2	3
Dressing	0	1	2	3
Balance/Gait	0	1	2	3
Transferring	0	1	2	3
Toileting	0	1	2	3
Taking Medications	0	1	2	3
Getting Emergency Help	0	1	2	3
Preparing Meals	0	1	2	3
Communication	0	1	2	3
Keeping Appointments	0	1	2	3
Bathing	0	1	2	3
Managing Finances	0	1	2	3
TOTAL				

<u>Total of 30 or Under</u> - A person with this score can still function independently.

<u>Total of 31-50</u> - A person with this score can perform some functions independently, but does require assistance in other areas. This person could benefit from regular in home assistance or moving to an assisted living facility.

Total of 51 or higher - A person with this score is no longer able to care for themselves independently, and they possibly have serious health issues. A nursing home or possibly a hospice service may be necessary to provide the care the individual requires at this stage.

Preparing for Medicaid

We always hope that a nursing home is not in our future, and rarely think about it until we are faced with the immediate need. As a caregiver, you understand your loved one may eventually need more care than you are able to provide. If that time comes, it will be very stressful. It is possible to do some organization in advance that will make the application process go more smoothly, and will also help you get your loved one's documents in order even if they don't ever need the nursing home.

One thing to keep in mind that there is a five year "lookback" for "transfers of assets" deemed to be made for the purpose of qualifying for Medicaid. This includes paying caregivers without a Medicaid qualifying contract. Any significant gifts made within five years of applying for Medicaid will need to be repaid or there will be a penalty period during which no Medicaid benefits will be available. An elder law attorney can assist you in this situation.

The items listed below are required for both spouses in the situation of a married couple. The "snapshot" date is the first day of admission to the hospital and/or nursing home for at least thirty continuous days.

- □ Driver's License or State ID
- □ Medicare Card
- □ Birth Certificate
- □ Marriage Certificate
- □ Guardianship Letters of Authority
- □ All information regarding rental property
- □ Statements of all assets as of Snapshot Date
- □ Copies of all savings bonds
- □ Current year's property tax bills
- □ Current year's Social Security Benefit letters
- □ Current Veteran's Benefits statements
- □ Any other income documentation
- □ Social Security Cards(s)
- □ Health Insurance Card(s)
- □ Naturalization Paperwork or Green Card
- □ Living Trust
- □ Durable Power of Attorney
- □ Deed(s) to all properties
- □ Current health insurance bill, if any
- □ All vehicle titles
- □ Current year's homeowner's insurance bill
- □ Current pension statements
- □ Current disability statements
- □ Life insurance face value and cash value

- ☐ Complete long term care insurance policy
- ☐ Complete annuity contracts
- ☐ Burial Plot paperwork
- ☐ Prepaid funeral paperwork
- ☐ Mortgage/equity loan/rent statement
- ☐ Condo fee statement

Asset Information

Must have documentary proof of the value

Institution	Type of Acct.	Acct. No.	Owner	Contact Info
	Checking			
	Checking			
	Checking			
	Savings			
	Savings			
	Savings			
	Money Market			
	Money Market			
	Money Market			
	CD			
	CD			
	CD			
	Savings Bonds			
	Life Insurance			
	Life Insurance			
	Life Insurance			
	IRA/401(k)			
	IRA/401(k)			
	Annuity			
	Annuity			

	Mutual Fund			
	Mutual Fund			
	Stock			

Resources

Adxcult Protective Services	(855) 444-3911
KPRO - The federal contractor Quality Improvement Organization that serves Michigan - 855-408-8557	Appeals of Discharge from Hospitals and Nursing Homes
Long Term Care Ombudsman 866-485-9393	Complaints about nursing homes or licensed assisted living facilities
Michigan Department of Community Health and Human Services	Complaint Intake
611 Ottawa St-Central Office P.O. Box 30664 Lansing, MI 48909	800-882-6006 http://www.michigan.gov/documents/lara/BCHS _Facility_Complaint_Form-361_517391_7.pdf
National Elder Law Foundation	Locate a Certified Elder Law Attorney
4700 S Thompson St, Springdale, AR 72764	www.nelf.org/findacela.asp
The Area Agencies on Aging are a federally assistance.	funded resource for aging information and
Region 1-A - Detroit Area on Aging	Serves Detroit, Hamtramck, Highland Park, Grosse Pointes, Harper Woods
1333 Brewery Park Blvd., Suite 400 Detroit, MI 48207	313-446-4444 https://www.detroitseniorsolution.org/
Region 1-B - Area Agency on Aging	Serves Counties of Livingston, Macomb, Monroe, Oakland, Washtenaw, St. Clair
29100 Northwestern Hwy., Suite 400 Southfield, MI 48034	248-357-2255 800-852-7795 www.aaa1b.org
Region 1-C - The Senior Alliance	Serves Western and Southern Wayne
5454 Venoy Rd, Wayne, MI 48184	734-722-2830 800-815-1112 www.aaa1c.org

Made in the USA
Monee, IL
04 November 2026

67378690R00021